P9-CQH-418

DEEPER
than
TEARS

J. Countryman is a registered trademark
of Word Publishing, Inc.

A J. Countryman Book

Designed by Koechel Peterson Inc.
Minneapolis, Minnesota

ISBN: 08499-1496-5

Printed in USA

DEEPER than TEARS

Promises of Comfort and Hope

WORD PUBLISHING

Dallas • London • Vancouver • Melbourne

Contents

PART I

TEARS

Thou hast often wiped away my tears,
restored peace to my mourning heart,
chastened me for my profit.
All thy work for me is perfect,
and I praise thee.

PURITAN PRAYER
The Valley of Vision

Victory

comes

through

defeat;

healing

through

brokenness;

finding self

through

losing self.

Charles Colson

What do we do when tragedy strikes? We hurt. We hurt when we have to confront the tragedy of divorce. We hurt when we have to face the tragedy that our children have become drug addicts. We hurt when we deal with the tragedy of bankruptcy. We hurt when we get the tragic news that the tumor is malignant and the prognosis is not good. We hurt when we experience the finality of a loved one's death.

But we also do something else—we turn to the deepest resources within us and draw upon the rudiments of our faith to sustain us.

PAUL WALKER
How to Keep Your Joy

> Count your
>
> night by
>
> stars, not
>
> shadows,
>
> Count your
>
> life with
>
> smiles, not
>
> tears.
>
> Italian Proverb

Because we live in a fallen world, life inevitably includes sorrow. When sin entered the human race, it brought death— physical death and spiritual death with all the accompanying ramifications. Death or loss of anything we value causes grief. However, God has a higher purpose for his people, and he is faithful to use our most painful times to mature us, to draw us into closer dependence on him.

VICKI KRAFT
Facing Your Feelings

Pain can be exhausting. Feelings of sorrow, depression, grief, and fear can eat away at us internally to the point that we feel our bodies will waste away.

We lose strength. We forfeit any sense of balance and control over our emotions. We're reduced to groaning, powerless, grief-stricken creatures.

Emotions are very fragile things. When you're working through old hurts or new struggles, your emotions can help you deal with them in a healthy way. Stuffing them, pretending you don't feel grief or fear, won't help at all. In fact, it will hurt you in the long run.

PETER WALLACE
*What the Psalmist Is
Saying to You Today*

My groaning has worn me out. At night my bed and pillow are soaked with tears.

Psalm 6:6

I know of only one
starting place in the war
against sorrow, and that
is . . . in the arms of
Almighty God.

Robert A. Williams

I, the LORD
your God,
will hold
your right
hand. . . .
Fear not, I
will help
you.

Isaiah 41:13

Grief, from whatever source, is a long and painful journey. And, I found, it is full of frightful choices. The urge to retreat into a cocoon-like existence is great, and depression is slipped into so easily. The allure of escaping into busyness or pleasurable fancies also raises its ugly head.

Alongside all of this temptation that would take us further and further from healing lies the sometimes obscure choice of acceptance. Obscure because this path leads into the pain and makes no promise of a quick cure. Instead, it opens the wound to its very depth and applies the healing balm of God's very special grace from the inside out.

VERDELL DAVIS
Riches Stored in Secret Places

Jesus was a strong man in a new way. He was at once very weak and very strong. He was not ashamed to shed tears over Jerusalem, whom he wanted to gather like a hen her chicks; he was not afraid to weep publicly at the raising of Lazarus; and he was not afraid to show his agony in Gethsemane. All this did not make for a "strong" man in the worldly sense. Yet Jesus' love was so strong that he was able to suffer the most terrible pain and godforsakenness, and in this strength he completed the task given him by his Father.

In true weakness we become powerless, and in true powerlessness we find strength. That is the secret.

J. HEINRICH ARNOLD
Discipleship

The grieving process is much like . . . surgery. When we allow the Great Physician to examine the issues of our lives, he may need to hold our hearts in his hands. What a vulnerable position to allow someone to scrutinize us that closely and find out what makes us tick. . . .

To become tenderhearted, insightful, and responsive to the Lord and others, we must first wade through our losses. That means a willingness to feel the effects of our loss, to examine our hearts under the tutelage of the Holy Spirit, to release tears, and to relinquish our rights to understand. In doing so, we will feel the pain, but we'll learn appropriate ways to express it. Sometimes it will be through the healing release of tears, prayer, some form of art, or words (spoken or written).

PATSY CLAIRMONT
Under His Wings

Though we know God is not to blame for any death, so many times it seems that he turns a blind eye by allowing his permissive will to occur. He stands dead-center when we are looking for a target. I'm convinced that God loves us so much that he is willing to take the blame, to absorb our anger when we need a punching bag. I think he would rather have us yelling at him than not speaking at all.

LESLIE WILLIAMS
Night Wrestling

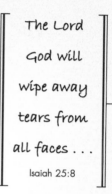

The Lord God will wipe away tears from all faces . . .

Isaiah 25:8

Grief is like a long valley, a winding valley where any bend may reveal a totally new landscape. . . . Not every bend does. Sometimes the surprise is the opposite one; you are presented with exactly the same sort of country you thought you had left behind miles ago. That is when you wonder whether the valley isn't a circular trench. But it isn't. There are partial recurrences, but the sequence doesn't repeat.

C. S. Lewis
A Grief Observed

We will always need other people and even more so in the darkening hours of personal tragedy.

Robert W. Williams

You can talk to God because God listens. Your voice matters in heaven. He takes you very seriously. When you enter his presence, the attendants turn to you to hear your voice. No need to fear that you will be ignored. Even if you stammer or stumble, even if what you have to say impresses no one, it impresses God—and he listens. . . .

Intently. Carefully. The prayers are honored as precious jewels. Purified and empowered, the words rise in a delightful fragrance to our Lord. . . . Your words do not stop until they reach the very throne of God.

MAX LUCADO
The Great House of God

Dear Risen Lord,

How hard it is to see clearly when devastating circumstances fill my eyes with tears. How blurry everything gets. Even you get blurry, and the sound of your voice becomes strangely unfamiliar.

Help me to blink away those tears to see that you are standing beside me, wanting to know why I am crying . . . wanting to know where it hurts . . . wanting to wipe away every tear from my eyes.

Thank you, Jesus, for being there, for never leaving me or forsaking me, even in the darkest and chilliest hours of my life.

KEN GIRE
Intimate Moments with the Savior

In all these things
we are more than
conquerors through
Him who loved us.

Romans 8:37

God longs to give us himself.
He longs to fill our lives with love
when we don't feel lovable

and grace when we can't take another step

and peace when the storm is raging about us

and joy when the tears of sadness are still on
our faces.

But we insist on running our own lives,
choosing pleasure or comfort or security over
the slower process of a changed life. And a
changed life always involves pain; it always
involves waiting; it always comes with the
temptation to seek the easy way out.

VERDELL DAVIS
Riches Stored in Secret Places

> God is the
> broken and
> God is the
> healer.
>
> Gloria Gaither

There are moments when the suffering is so deep that one can hardly talk to a person. What a joy it is then to know that the Lord understands. No pit is so deep that the Lord is not deeper still. Underneath us are the everlasting arms—and the Lord understands.

> He shall cover thee with
>   his feathers,
> and under his wings shalt
>   thou trust:
> his truth shall be thy
>   shield and buckler.
>
> *Psalm 91:4*

CORRIE TEN BOOM
He Cares, He Comforts

Grieving is a process, not an address. Because we have experienced loss doesn't mean we should set up house with it. When we're willing to let the Lord do some internal surgery and then work through the recovery time, we will eventually enter the lighter and brighter season of spring.

PATSY CLAIRMONT
Under His Wings

Weeping may last for the night, but a shout of joy comes in the morning.

Psalm 30:5
NASB.

27

> Human friends can weep with us when we weep; but Jesus is a friend, who when He has wept with us, can wipe away all our tears.
>
> William Nevins

As people navigate each stage of grief, the principle for a successful journey is the same: grief needs to be expressed. Grief resembles steam in an engine. Unless the steam can escape in a controlled manner, pressure builds up and the boiler explodes. Grief work, too, must be done. It will be done. . . .

A good listener gives the grief sufferer permission to express thoughts and feelings by asking, "Tell me how things are." Or, "Would you like to talk about it?"

HADDON W. ROBINSON
Grief

Someone once said that the greatest part of grief is regret. Regret includes sorrow and remorse, and has to do with unfinished business this side of the grave. Since those of us still living on earth cannot experience Paradise except in brief glints, part of our task after someone we love dies is to clean up the regrets. Because regret is a many-pronged thing (remorse over something we did or didn't do, sorrow that time with the loved one was cut short, regret that the dying one suffered), the main component of regret, as well as the ticket for working through it is forgiveness. For us who are left behind, we must forgive others for the circumstances of the death, forgive the loved one for leaving us, and forgive ourselves for an imperfect relationship with the one who died.

LESLIE WILLIAMS
Night Wrestling

The reactions of grief are
not like recipes,
with given ingredients,
and certain results.

Each person mourns in
a different way. . . .

Grief is universal.
At the same time it
is extremely personal.

EARL A. GROLLMAN
Living When a Loved One Has Died

> Buried under the biggest burden is a good place to find an even bigger blessing.
>
> Janette Oke

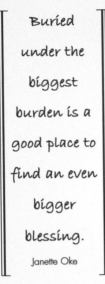

If you are experiencing grief for any reason, allow yourself time to mourn and weep. If you try to hold in your tears and ignore your pain, there may be serious problems later. God gave us tears to shed in our grief, an outpouring of our inner pain.

When we are hurting, there are two extremes to avoid. One extreme is to block our emotions, determined that we will never care so much that we can be hurt that way again. It is unhealthy to block our emotions to protect ourselves. . . . The other extreme is to become so consumed by our grief that nothing else matters. The best thing to do is to get back into the normal process of life again.

VICKI KRAFT
Facing Your Feelings

Our lives are like plotlines in a novel, with God as the Author. In literary terms, I have heard it said that there is no such thing as a Christian tragedy because, though tragic things may happen to the Protagonist, the Christian always ends up in the arms of God.

Death is not the last word. Disaster only brings the Christian closer to God. Nasty surprises or twists and turns of plot do not deter us from the path we tread. Because of the cross, we may march through earthly jungles, deserts, gardens, cities, but we are on a heavenly trek. No matter what our journeys lead us through, we always end up in God. From where we stand now, our future may look dreadful, exciting, boring, but we may rest assured that we are in better hands than our own if we simply give our future to Christi.

LESLIE WILLIAMS
Night Wrestling

PART II

TENDERNESS—

May I never forget

That thou hast my heart

in thy hands.

PURITAN PRAYER
The Valley of Vision

Some of you who read these pages are in the process of having every crutch removed from your life. This creates enormous pain and instability when support we had counted on is torn from us.

For some, it is represented by a broken romance. The man or woman you felt was God's choice has now vanished, and it hurts deeply. . . .

For some it has been the death of a dream. Everything you hoped and planned for has gone up in smoke.

Now, you have a choice. You can look around for some other something or someone to lean on—or you can lean on God, and God ALONE.

CHARLES SWINDOLL
David

Passage through the darkness of doubts and crises . . . is essential to growth in the process of faith.

John Powell

In the midst of your daily storms, make it a point to be still and set your sights on [God]. Let God be God. Let him bathe you in his glory so that your breath and your troubles are sucked from your soul. Be still. Be quiet. Be open and willing. Then you will know that God is God.

MAX LUCADO
The Great House of God

Can strength be born out of weakness? Courage out of fear? Joy out of sorrow? Confidence out of feelings of inadequacy? Compassion out of pain? New life out of loss? . . .

When we stand in the middle of a lifestorm, it seems as if the storm has become our way of life. We cannot see a way out. We are unable to chart a course back to smoother waters. We feel defeated—and broken. Will that brokenness produce a cynicism that will keep us forever in the mire of "if only" thinking? Or will we yield up that brokenness to the resources of One who calms the winds and the waves, heals the brokenhearted, and forgives the most grievous of sins? The choice is ours.

VERDELL DAVIS
Riches Stored in Secret Places

Jesus, thou art all compassion,

Pure unbounded love thou art;

Visit us with thy salvation,

Enter every trembling heart.

Charles Wesley
1707–1788

> What happens to good people when bad things happen to them? They become better people.
>
> Robert Schuller

 God's love is Forever Love. It's the kind you can abide in and not wonder if it will still be there when you wake up. God's love is as solid as the wooden cross that was set into the ground of Golgotha, as solid as the nails that were driven into the flesh of his hands, as solid as the rock that was rolled away from his tomb.

You are loved. Stick that in your heart and abide in it.

LIZ CURTIS HIGGS
Reflecting His Image

God has been intimately acquainted with each human soul since the beginning of time. He looks upon the world and sees billions of individuals, one at a time. Each heart, each mind, each soul—he knows them personally. Intimately. Because he fashioned each one individually.

So when your heart is full of joy, bursting with pleasure over an accomplishment or a deepened relationship or a conquered hurt, he feels it, too.

And when your heart hurts because someone has wounded it or you've disappointed yourself by the way you acted, he feels that, too.

Out of the billions of other souls in the world, God sees you. He knows you. He loves you. And he's willing and able to help you.

PETER WALLACE
*What the Psalmist Is
Saying to You Today*

When a person reacts positively to tragedy—that's a miracle. Psalm 23 concludes with the glorious line: "Surely goodness and mercy shall follow me all the days of my life." That's God's way of saying that life will often be filled with goodness, but that even when God's goodness cannot be seen, his mercy can be experienced! In the midst of tears, heartbreak, enormous loss, and terrible sorrow, suddenly a sweet mood, like a gentle kiss, will touch your wounded heart. That experience is called mercy. It comes as an expression of God's love.

The good news I have for you is: God promises mercy adequate enough to meet any tragedy.

ROBERT SCHULLER
The Be Happy Attitudes

Save me,
O God, for
the waters
have come up
to my neck.

Psalm 69:1–3

Why is it so hard to believe Christ and trust him completely? Christ wants to give us his life and spirit, and if we look to him for only a moment, our hearts tell us: Here is one we can trust. Yet each of us knows feelings of fear and anxiety. Something in us seeks Christ, and at the same time something in us wants to serve self and is unwilling to surrender to him completely. But that is what we must do, for the Gospel says "trust and believe."

J. Heinrich Arnold
Discipleship

SPEAK TO HIM

Speak to Him thou for He hears,
and Spirit with Spirit can meet—
  Closer is He than breathing,
  and nearer than hands and feet.

ALFRED, LORD TENNYSON
1809–1892

Our God, our help in ages past,

Our hope for years to come,

Be thou our guard while troubles last,

And our eternal home.

Isaac Watts
1674–1748

> Lo, I am with you alway, even unto the end of the world.
>
> Matthew 28:20

 "What a Friend we have in Jesus!" His hand keeps us, not only when we go through the valley of the shadow of death but also before that. When we pray, "Take my hand, Lord, and hold me tight," the Lord does it. . . .

My father used to say to us, when we were children and had to go away from home for a while, "Children, don't forget, when Jesus takes your hand, then he holds you tight. And when Jesus keeps you tight, he guides you through life. And when Jesus guides you through life, one day he brings you safely home."

CORRIE TEN BOOM
He Cares, He Comforts

Sometimes the materials [God] provides are things of beauty, . . . and sometimes they are things which break our hearts— not gifts in the sense that Almighty God decrees the evil and suffering of the world (we only know *that* he allowed it, we do not know *why*), but gifts in that he gives to us himself—his presence, his never-failing love in the midst of our pain.

We may offer up those very pains, those inexplicable catastrophes that baffle us to silence. We may even give him our broken hearts, for the sacrifices of God, we are told, are "a broken, spirit, a broken and a contrite heart." All of it— the gladness and the sorrow—material for sacrifice, given "day by day without fail."

For one who has made thanksgiving the habit of his life, the morning prayer will be, "Lord, what will you give me today to offer back to you?"

ELISABETH ELLIOT
Love Has a Price Tag

The God of all comfort does not seem to extend his comfort to make us comfortable. Perhaps that's because our tendency would be to become La-Z-Boy believers, content to crank back our chairs, put up our feet, and snooze through the losses of others. Instead, he offers his comfort that we might be motivated by mercy to tenderly extend kindness to the hurting. . . .

If we don't feel, weep, talk, rage, grieve, and question, we will hide and be afraid of the parts of life that deepen us. They make us not only wiser but also gentler, more compassionate, less critical, and more Christlike.

PATSY CLAIRMONT
Under His Wings

There is not enough darkness in all the world to put out the light of one small candle . . . .

This inscription was found on a small, new gravestone after a devastating air raid on Britain in World War II. Some thought it must be a famous quotation, but it wasn't. The words were written by a lonely old lady whose pet had been killed by a Nazi bomb.

I have always remembered those words, not so much for their poetry and imagery as for the truth they contain. In moments of discouragement, defeat or even despair, there are always certain things to cling to. Little things, usually: remembered laughter, the face of a sleeping child, a tree in the wind—in fact, any reminder of something deeply felt or dearly loved.

No man is so poor as not to have many of these small candles. When they are lighted, darkness goes away . . . and a touch of wonder remains.

ARTHUR GORDON
A Touch of Wonder

I Shall Know Why

I shall know why, when time is over,
And I have ceased to wonder why;
Christ will explain each separate anguish
In the fair schoolroom of the sky.

Emily Dickinson
1830–1886

PART III

TRIALS—

Help me to see that although
I am in the wilderness
it is not all briars and barrenness.
I have—bread from heaven,
streams from the rock,
light by day, fire by night,
thy dwelling place and thy mercy seat.
I am sometimes discouraged by the way,
but though winding and trying,
it is safe and short.

PURITAN PRAYER
The Valley of Vision

The master musician knows that suffering precedes glory and acclaim. He knows the hours, days, and months of grueling practice and self-sacrifice that precede the one hour of perfect rendition when his efforts are applauded. The master craftsman knows that years of work, sacrifice, and suffering as an apprentice precede his being promoted to the master of his trade. The student knows that years of study, self-denial, and commitment precede the triumphant day of graduation with honors. . . .

The Bible teaches that suffering is a part of life in a sinful world. Paul said, "For I reckon that the sufferings of this present time are not worthy to be compared with the glory which shall be revealed in us" (Romans 8:18).

BILLY GRAHAM
Unto the Hills

During Jesus' three years as an itinerant rabbi, he knew what it was to be weary, hungry, and homeless. . . . He was praised and scorned, followed and forsaken, loved and hated, listened to and rejected, crowned and crucified. He had every reason to feel lonely in the world of men, but it was thus that he "learned" and demonstrated for us the meaning of obedience—through the things that he suffered. . . .

To walk with him is to walk the Way of the Cross. If the cross we are asked to take up is not presented to us in the form of martyrdom, heroic action of some kind, dragons or labyrinths or even "ministry"—at least something that looks spiritual—are we to conclude that he has waived the requirement?

He never waives the requirement.

ELISABETH ELLIOT
The Path of Loneliness

Doesn't faith dry all tears? Religious people sometimes mishandle their own grief and the grief of others by thinking that faith and tears don't mix. A sturdy faith in God and a firm belief in the promise of life eternal, they reason, should keep us from weeping or giving way to grief. But grief is not a denial of faith. The shortest verse in the Bible is found in John 11:35. It states simply: "Jesus wept."

HADDON W. ROBINSON
Grief

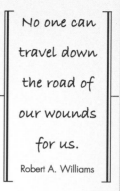

No one can travel down the road of our wounds for us.

Robert A. Williams

How many of us get into a panic when we are faced by physical desolation, by death, or war, injustice, poverty, disease? All these in all their force will never turn to panic the one who believes in the absolute sovereignty of his Lord.

The thing that preserves a man from panic is his relationship to God: if he is only related to himself and to his own courage, there may come a moment when his courage gives out.

Don't be disturbed today by thoughts about tomorrow; leave tomorrow alone, and bank in confidence on God's organizing of what you do not see.

OSWALD CHAMBERS
Run Today's Race

Most of us would not mind being a saint; we just do not want to take the course for sainthood. We wouldn't mind coming out gold; we just don't want to go through the refiner's fire. And being like clay in the potter's hand doesn't appeal to us too much either. We might opt for being great if we just didn't have to *become* great.

And so we settle for the little village at the foot of the trail instead of climbing the torturous trail to the summit. . . . But to choose, anywhere along the way, not to endure the pain of the climb is to miss the grandeur of the mountain peak.

None of us goes into the refiner's fire or onto the potter's wheel in total submission. We hold onto whatever comforts we have and cry for peace, not perfection.

VERDELL DAVIS
Riches Stored in Secret Places

O Love that wilt not let me go,

I rest my weary soul in Thee;

I give Thee back the life I owe,

That in Thine ocean depths its flow

May richer, fuller be.

George Matheson

The hidden wounds you carry with you today—those private hurts that you can't talk about—what were the weapons that inflicted them on your heart? . . .

Someone turned his or her back on you, didn't return your gesture of love and friendship, and that hurt. . . . You were rebuffed. Words, looks, actions—these are the horrible weapons that inflict hidden wounds in human hearts.

Now the question is, *What do we do with these hidden wounds? How do we handle them?*

Don't nurse the wound. Don't curse the wound. Don't keep rehearsing the wounding experience. What do you do with your hidden wounds? Immerse them. Drown them in a life of noble service.

ROBERT SCHULLER
The Be Happy Attitudes

ON ANOTHER'S SORROW

Can I see another's woe,
And not be in sorrow too?
Can I see another's grief,
And not seek for kind relief?
Can I see a falling tear,
And not feel my sorrow's share?
Can a father see his child
Weep, nor be with sorrow fill'd?

WILLIAM BLAKE
1757–1827

A Trojan horse sits just outside the gate of your heart. Its name is bitterness. It is a monument to every attack you have endured from your fellow human beings. It is a gift left by the people who have wronged you. . . .

But to accept the gift is to invite ruin into your life. You see, there is more to the horse than meets the eye. The feeling of justification it brings is the deceptive artistry of a master craftsman. Though decorated with the promise of vindication, it is only a lure. The celebration is short-lived. Once inside the walls of your heart, it releases its agents of destruction. Its plot quietly unfolds from the inside out. To become a person of character, you must learn to recognize the Trojan horse of bitterness. And more important, you must never bring it inside. . . . The only remedy is forgiveness.

ANDY STANLEY
Like a Rock

> I praise you, LORD, for being my guide. Even in the darkest night, your teachings fill my mind.
>
> —Psalm 16:7

Life throws us curves all the time. And forks in the road. And roadblocks. In those times, we turn to the Lord for direction. And in his time, in his way, he gives it if we can hear it.

Sometimes we have to wait until the night to hear it. When things seem darkest, coldest, and emptiest, the truth can burst through.

God's guidance shows the way that leads to true life. It is always for our good. And it will always come when we need it most.

Wait for God, even if the night seems dark. He will give you everything you need when you need it. It may not be what you want or expect, but it is the best.

PETER WALLACE
What the Psalmist Is Saying to You Today

All you want is an open door or an extra day or an answered prayer, for which you will be thankful.

And so you pray and wait.

No answer.

You pray and wait.

No answer. . . .

May I ask a very important question? What if God says no?

What if the request is delayed or even denied? When God says no to you, how will you respond? If God says, "I've given you my grace, and that is enough," will you be content?

MAX LUCADO
In the Grip of Grace

Hear me, o LORD,

for Your loving

kindness is good. . . .

Psalm 69:16

When we feel stuck in a dark room of doubt, or pain, or discomfort, or angst, Satan sometimes tempts us to think we will be in this miserable place forever. Then God reminds us of tomorrow. The future is like a long, black corridor with light shining dimly under the door. Though we may feel alone, locked in one of the rooms off the hallway, we can hear the passing of feet, and we can pray to God to unlock the door and to walk with us toward the slim band of light visible just ahead.

The ability to project past the present pain gives us hope and endurance, leading us toward the light of a better day.

LESLIE WILLIAMS
Night Wrestling

All of us have wondered at times why God doesn't do more to fix our problems. But our human eyes often fail to see that God isn't rushing to change our circumstances because he is concerned with a much more serious problem—our character.

While you struggle with the woes of this world, God's main occupation is preparing you for the world to come. The focus of what God is doing in your life takes place *in* you, not *around* you.

ANDY STANLEY
Like a Rock

> Look at what you have left in your life; never look at what you have lost.
>
> Robert Schuller

One of the most famous books ever written was written by a man who was serving his third term in prison. The book he wrote has changed the lives of literally millions of people. The man was John Bunyan, and the book is *The Pilgrim's Progress.*

At one point in this story, while Pilgrim is making the long, arduous journey to the City of God, he falls into a deep, miry, muddy hole called the Slough of Despond. He cannot get out by himself, but when he begins to cry out, Help—a picture of the Holy Spirit—reaches down and lifts him up from his despondency.

If we were to translate Bunyan's Slough of Despond into today's terms, we would call that muddy hole "the pits." . . .

There is nothing ethically, morally, or spiritually wrong with our experiencing cloudy days and dark nights. They are inevitable. That's why James says, "Consider it all joy WHEN you encounter various trials" (James. 1:2).

CHARLES SWINDOLL
David

Affliction can be a means of refining and of purification. Many a life has come forth from the furnace of affliction more beautiful and more useful. We might never have had the songs of Fanny Crosby had she not been afflicted with blindness. . . . The "Hallelujah Chorus" was written by Handel when he was poverty-stricken and suffering from a paralyzed right side and right arm.

David said, "Before I was afflicted I went astray: but now have I kept thy word" (Psalm 119:67). We learn through the trials we are called upon to bear.

BILLY GRAHAM
Unto the Hills

Nature is God's workshop The sky is his résumé. The universe is his calling card. You want to know who God is? See what he has done. You want to know his power? Take a look at his creation. Curious about his strength? Pay a visit to his home address: 1 Billion Starry Sky Avenue. Want to know his size? Step out into the night and stare at starlight emitted one million years ago. . . .

What controls you doesn' t control him. What troubles you doesn't trouble him. What fatigues you doesn't fatigue him. . . . "What is impossible with man is possible with God" (Matt. 19:26).

MAX LUCADO
The Great House of God

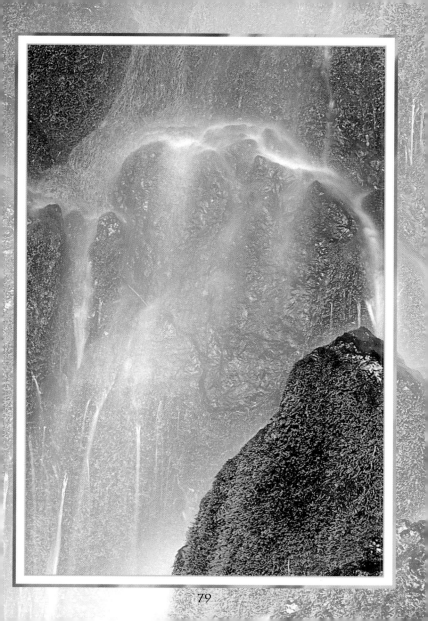

TRUST—

Help me, O Lord, to throw
myself absolutely
and wholly on thee,
for better, for worse, without
comfort, and all but hopeless.

PURITAN PRAYER
The Valley of Vision

Like sunshine over a valley, God's great love spreads out over the whole earth. It is true that there are terrible things in the world, such as war; and wars will come, but God is greater. He is much greater than man, and his love is much greater than man's. Do not live in fear. Look down across the valley and toward the mountains, and think of the great God who created all things, and who has you in his hand.

If we live according to Jesus and his teachings. we have no reason to be afraid. Let us be faithful to him and to God and leave all fear behind.

Learn to trust Jesus always, even when you cannot understand something.

J. HEINRICH ARNOLD
Discipleship

Discouragement is a large cloud that, like all clouds, obscures the warmth and joy of the sun. In the case of spiritual discouragement, the Son of God, the Lord Jesus, is eclipsed in our lives. Discouragement is Satan's device to thwart the work of God in our lives. Discouragement blinds our eyes to the mercy of God and makes us perceive only the unfavorable circumstances.

There is only one way to dispel discouragement, and it is not in our own strength or ingenuity. The Bible says, "Wait on the Lord: be of good courage, and he shall strengthen thine heart: wait, I say on the Lord" (Psalm 27:14).

BILLY GRAHAM
Unto the Hills

The loss of someone we love, whether by death or otherwise, brings us to the brink of the abyss of mystery. If we wrestle, as most of us are forced to do, with the question of God in the matter, we are bound to ask why he found it necessary to withdraw such a good gift. We will not get the whole answer, but certainly one answer is the necessity of being reminded that wherever our treasure is there will our hearts be also. If we have put all our eggs in the basket of earthly life and earthly affections we haven't much left when the basket falls. Christians, being citizens of Another Country, subjects of a Heavenly King, are supposed to set their affections there rather than here—a lesson few learn without mortal anguish.

ELISABETH ELLIOT
The Path of Loneliness

Trust in the Lord with
all your heart, and
lean not on your own
understanding.

Proverbs 3:5

Lord, I have been so defeated by circumstances. I have felt like an animal trapped in a corner with nowhere to flee. Where are *You* in all this, Lord? The night is dark. I cannot feel Your presence.

Help me to know that the darkness is really "Shade of Your hand, outstretched caressingly"; that the "hemming in" is Your doing. Perhaps there was no other way You could get my full attention, no other way I would allow You to demonstrate what You can do in my life.

I see now that the emptier my cup is, the more space there is to receive Your love and supply.

CATHERINE MARSHALL
Adventures in Prayer

JOY AND PEACE IN BELIEVING

Sometimes a light surprises
The Christian while he sings;
It is the Lord who rises
With healing on His wings.
When comforts are declining,
He grants the soul again
A season of clear shining
To cheer it after rain.

WILLIAM COWPER
1731–1800

In our own spiritual experience some terror comes down the road to meet us and our hearts are seized with a tremendous fear; then we hear our own name called, and the voice of Jesus saying, "It is I, be not afraid," and the peace of God which passeth all understanding takes possession of our hearts.

Experiences of what God has done for me are only stepping-stones; the one great note is— I trust in the Lord Jesus. God's providence can do with me what it likes, make the heavens like brass, earth like hell, my body loathsome (as Job's was), but the soul that is trusting in Jesus gets where Job got, "Though He slay me, yet will I trust Him."

OSWALD CHAMBERS
Run Today's Race

When you are confused about the future, go to your *Jehovah-roi*, your caring shepherd. When you are anxious about provision, talk to *Jehovah-jireh*, the Lord who provides. Are your challenges too great? Seek the help of *Jehovah-shalom*, the Lord is peace. Is your body sick? Are your emotions weak? *Jehovah-rophe*, the Lord who heals you, will see you now. Do you feel like a soldier stranded behind enemy lines? Take refuge in *Jehovah-nissi*, the Lord my banner.

Meditating on the names of God reminds you of the character of God. Take these names and bury them in your heart. God is
the shepherd who guides,
the Lord who provides,
the voice who brings peace in the storm,
the physician who heals the sick,
and the banner that guides the soldier.

And most of all, he . . . is.

MAX LUCADO
The Great House of God

The very best prescription for banishing worry is found in Psalm 37:5: "Commit thy way unto the Lord; trust also in him; and he shall bring it to pass."

Think of the things you do not worry about. Perhaps you never worry about whether you will be able to get water out of the faucet in your kitchen, or maybe you do not worry about a tree falling on your house.

Now ask yourself why you do not worry about such things. Is it because, in the case of running water, that it has always been there every time you wanted it, or that a tree has never fallen on your house before? Certainty breeds trust, doesn't it?

We can be just as certain and just as worry-free about God's love, protection, and provision because he has never gone back on a single one of his promises. He never changes. Great is his faithfulness.

BILLY GRAHAM
Unto the Hills

We have been shown the way of acceptance on every page of the life of Jesus. It sprang from love and from trust. He set his face like a flint toward Jerusalem. He took up the Cross of his own will. No one could take his life from him. He deliberately laid it down. He calls us to take up our crosses. That is a different thing from capitulation or resignation. It is a glad and voluntary YES to the conditions we meet on our journey with him, because these are the conditions he wants us to share with him. Events are the *sacraments* of the Will of God—that is, they are visible signs of an invisible Reality. These provide the very place where we may learn to love and trust. Heaven waits for our response.

ELISABETH ELLIOT
The Path of Loneliness

> The richest
> source of
> healing our
> loneliness is
> for us to
> begin to give
> ourselves
> in love.
>
> Robert A. Williams

 God is doing a greater work in us, and that can only come as we learn to trust him no matter how dark the days and sleepless the nights. And it is only as we have been through the darkness with him that what we know with our heads slides down into our hearts, and our hearts no longer demand answers. The Why? becomes unimportant when we believe that God can and will redeem the pain for our good and his glory. . . .

When I put the sovereignty of God beside his unfailing love, my heart can rest.

VERDELL DAVIS
Riches Stored in Secret Places

People who walk closely, steadily with God do not fear the future.

Even when bad news comes, they can accept it. That doesn't mean they won't have emotions about it—sadness, anger, even despair. But they know there is no need to fear, even in the face of disaster, because they trust God.

They know God is in control of all things. God can work all things for the good. So when even terrible circumstances erupt around them, their immediate reaction is to jump into God's arms and let him carry them.

PETER WALLACE
*What the Psalmist Is Saying
to You Today*

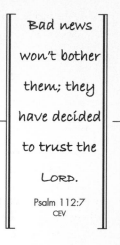

Bad news won't bother them; they have decided to trust the LORD.

Psalm 112:7
CEV

There is someone who hears our hearts and understands even our unformed thoughts. Christ is that one. He woos us, and he waits for us to come to him. With arms outstretched like open wings, he welcomes us. In this life we need a hiding place, and Christ offers us that—a place of comfort, a place of healing, but not a place of painlessness.

There will come a day for each of us when . . . we will reside where he presides and hiding won't be necessary, for we will be home . . . at last. Finally, we will be in a place where our tears will dry, our pain will pass, our hearts will heal, and we won't ever need to hide again—not from ourselves, not from each other, and, hallelujah, not from the One who knows us the best and loves us the most.

PATSY CLAIRMONT
Under His Wings

Rock of Ages,
cleft for me,
Let me hide myself
in Thee!

Augustus Montague Toplady
1740-1778

Though we may feel as though we move through a labyrinth, we are being led by a power greater than ourselves. The solution to the original labyrinth was to walk through the maze using a string tied to the opening to avoid getting lost. In the Christian journey, the Holy Spirit is the string, guiding us through the confusing corridors of life.

Undergirding each of the choices we make in life, God is leading us. In our ignorance or in our false desires, we may make what we think is the "wrong" choice; however, because of God's redemption on the cross, there are no ultimate "wrong" choices. God redeems all our blunders, all our stupidity. The crucial choice is choosing God over not choosing God.

Our job is to hold tight to the string.

LESLIE WILLIAMS
Night Wrestling

God would have us trust him.
Just trust him.

Trust him to know our way much better than we ever could. . . .

Trust him to give us the light we need. . . .

Trust him to be there in our darkness.

In teaching us to walk by faith and not by sight, God is placing down deep inside of us the resources we will need when darkness overtakes our journey. But more, he is seeking to forge in us a faith that will, in turn, make us lights to others in the sadness of their journey.

VERDELL DAVIS
Riches Stored in Secret Places

TRIUMPH—

Give me a mountain top

as high as the valley is low.

All-wise God,

Your never-failing providence

orders every event,

sweetens every fear. . . .

Out of my sorrow and night . . .

help me to love thee as thy child.

PURITAN PRAYER
In the Valley of Vision

At the edge of a rocky overlook in the Appalachian foothills stands a lone two-hundred-year-old evergreen tree. . . . Through the years, it has defied heavy snows, hailstorms, and the steady, westerly winds rising off the valley floor. From its vulnerable view of endless ridges and valleys, it has seen conditions that would snap most trees in half. Nevertheless, it stands strong.

What's the secret? . . . The answer lies below the surface. For literally two centuries, the elements have hurled their assaults against the tree. But while storms raged on the outside, the tree was quietly developing an inner support system to sustain it. Every gust of wind sent the roots sprawling deeper into the soil, expanding the tree's tenacious grip on the mountain. . . .

We are all like trees subjected to the stormy elements of life. And when they come, we either snap or grow stronger. What makes the difference is not the ferocity of the storm but the depth of our character.

ANDY STANLEY
Like a Rock

Stand still,
and whisper
God's name,
and listen.
He is nearer
than you
think.

Max Lucado

 Why does God bring thunderclouds and disasters when we want green pastures and still waters? Bit by bit we find behind the clouds, the Father's feet; behind the lightning, an abiding day that has no night; behind the thunder, "a still small voice" that comforts with a comfort that is unspeakable.

OSWALD CHAMBERS
Run Today's Race

The way I respond to the "givens" in my daily experience determines my growth in holiness. When we pray, "Give us this day our daily bread," God answers that prayer, measuring out just what we need for spiritual as well as physical growth. He knows that spiritual stamina cannot develop without conflict. We must take with both hands the thing given, submissively, humbly, sometimes courageously, or even, as one friend put it, "defiantly"—saying to ourselves, *This is part of the story*, the story of the love of God for me and of my love for him.

This is acceptance in the truest sense. This is where real peace is found—that strange, inexplicable peace Jesus promised.

ELISABETH ELLIOTT
The Path of Loneliness

Surely he hath

borne our griefs

and carried

our sorrows. . . .

Isaiah 53:4

The stone beside me marked the resting place of somebody's BELOVED WIFE who died in 1865 of A FEVER. Beneath her name was a line of script, almost indistinguishable. I looked closer, wondering which biblical phrase her grieving children might have chosen. But it was not a quotation; it was a statement: EVER SHE SOUGHT THE BEST, EVER FOUND IT.

Eight words. I stood there with my fingers on the cool stone, feeling the present fade and the past stir behind the illusion we call time. A century ago this woman had been living through a hideous war. Perhaps it took her husband from her, perhaps her sons. When it ended her country was beaten, broken, impoverished. She must have known humiliation, tasted despair. Yet someone who knew her had written that she always looked for the best, and always found it.

ARTHUR GORDON
A Touch of Wonder

To know that I have helped [someone] a little or made a day brighter will make my own work easier and cause the sun to shine on the dark days, for we all have them.

'Tis then a little place of sunshine in the heart helps mightily. And there is nothing that puts so much brightness there as having helped someone else.

LAURA INGALLS WILDER
Words from a Fearless Heart

What you look for in life . . . you will surely find. But the direction in which you look is up to you.

Arthur Gordon

Those whose lives have had the deepest spiritual impact in the world are those who have suffered. In God's mysterious providence, the Cross and the crown, suffering and glory are linked. . . .

Out of suffering comes holiness—in these forms: comfort, consolation, the fellowship of Christ's suffering, salvation, strength, fortitude, endurance. This is what is meant by redemptive suffering. The greater the measure allotted to us, the greater is our material for sacrifice. As we make it a joyful offering to God, our potential is enhanced for becoming "instruments of His peace"—being "broken bread and poured-out wine," overflowing with consolation for the lonely and the suffering of the world.

ELISABETH ELLIOT
The Path of Loneliness

God *is* for you. Not "may be," not "has been," not "was," not "would be," but "God is!" He *is* for you. Today. At this hour. At this minute. As you read this sentence. No need to wait in line or come back tomorrow. He is with you. He could not be closer than he is at this second. His loyalty won't increase if you are better nor lessen if you are worse. He is for you. . . .

God is for *you*. Had he a calendar, your birthday would be circled. If he drove a car, your name would be on his bumper. If there's a tree in heaven, he's carved your name in the bark. We know he has a tattoo, and we know what it says. "I have written your name on my hand," . . . (Isa. 49:16).

MAX LUCADO
In the Grip of Grace

> God
> clears the
> underbrush
> ahead and
> guides us . . .
> through
> thickets of
> time and
> uncertainty.
>
> Leslie Williams

The thing I keep trying to remember about giving the future over to God is that, like control, it belongs to him anyway. Through blindness or selfishness, I can stumble around trying my best to ruin God's plan for my life, but as long as I am living in him, the future takes care of itself, no matter what I do. If God is the Destination of our spiritual journey, then we are freed from the fear of making bad choices. The present moment is all that matters. The future snuggles right into the present, and gives us peace.

LESLIE WILLIAMS
Night Wrestling

Peace is much less a condition than a state of mind. Anxiety and tension can rule the day even when the circumstances of my life would indicate that all should be well with me. I can walk in sunshine and see only the shadows. I can be surrounded by those I love and be consumed with fear of losing them. I can accomplish a great task and still wonder why I did not do better. . . .

Peace, in the ultimate meaning of the word, is not the absence of conflict. It is not the accumulation of wealth, or comfort and ease, or a state of happiness. Peace is that sense down deep inside that says no matter what happens, all is well with my soul.

VERDELL DAVIS
Riches Stored in Secret Places

Look up. Lift up your head. Open your eyes and look around you. And praise the Lord.

That can be a tough thing to do at times. When we focus on the frustrations of life, the pain of fractured relationships past and present, the powerlessness we often feel over our circumstances, the last thing we feel like doing is praising the Lord.

But David the psalmist encourages us to let go of all that weight of our existence and look at God. Recognize his power and authority, his magnificence and excellence, his glory and light. He is all and in all and over all including all those things that tend to keep our eyes off him.

PETER WALLACE
*What the Psalmist
Is Saying to You Today*

> When we are in despair, God gives us the courage to go on.
>
> Robert Schuller

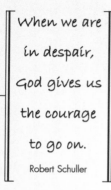

 No matter what the circumstances, God always has the last word. Always. And it is a word of triumph. There is no death! What joy! For those of us still left on earth puzzling it out, ultimately, after weeping through the night, we notice that the shades lighten slowly, and sunlight eventually pours in, making the dust motes dance, and making the room habitable once again.

The peace of God passes understanding.

LESLIE WILLIAMS
Night Wrestling

"JESUS HEARD YOU . . . ."

Jesus heard when you prayed last night.
He talked with God about you.
Jesus was there when you fought
    your fight,
he is going to bring you through.

Jesus knew when you shed those tears,
you did not weep alone.
The burdens you thought too heavy
    to bear,
he made them his very own.

Jesus himself was touched by that trial,
you could not understand.
Jesus stood by as you almost fell
and lovingly clasped your hand.

Jesus cared when you bore that pain,
indeed, he bore it too.
He felt each pain, each ache in
    your heart,
because of his love for you.

CORRIE TEN BOOM
He Cares, He Comforts

Blessed are you who weep now, for you shall laugh. (Luke 6:21)

The courage to laugh ultimately rests with our belief in the faithfulnss of God. During our grief we will not likely laugh for the right reasons, unless we feel assured that God has a stake in our lives and will come through for us. So then, it becomes our belief behind our laughter that makes the laughter a healing force. God himself has engendered our laughter, and he becomes the divine enabler of our joy.

ROBERT A. WILLIAMS
Journey Through Grief

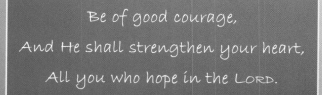

Be of good courage,

And He shall strengthen your heart,

All you who hope in the LORD.

Psalm 31:24

ACKNOWLEDGMENTS

Grateful acknowledgment is made to the following publishers and copyright holders for permission to reprint copyrighted material:

J. Heinrich Arnold, *Discipleship:Living for Christ in the Daily Grind* (Farmington, Penn.: ©1994 The Plough Publishing House.)

Arthur Bennett, ed., *The Valley of Vision* (Carlisle, Penn.: The Banner of Truth Trust, 1995).

Corrie ten Boom, *He Cares, He Comforts* (Grand Rapids, Mich.: Fleming H. Revell Co., 1977).

Patsy Clairmont, *Under His Wings and other Places of Refuge* (Colorado Springs, Colo.: Focus on the Family, ©1994 Patsy Clairmont).

Oswald Chambers, *Run Today's Race* (Grand Rapids, Mich.: Discovery House Publishers, ©1968 by the Oswald Chambers Pub. Assn. Ltd. and is used by permission of Discovery House Publishers).

Verdell Davis, *Riches Stored in Secret Places* (Dallas, Tex.: Word Publishing, 1994).

Elisabeth Elliot, *Love Has a Price Tag* (1979 Servant Publications , Box 8617, Ann Arbor, Michigan 48107).

Elisabeth Elliot, *The Path of Loneliness* (Nashville, Tenn.: Thomas Nelson, 1988).

Ken Gire, *Intimate Moments with the Savior* (Grand Rapids, Mich.: Zondervan, ©1989 by Ken Gire).

Arthur Gordon, *A Touch of Wonder* (Grand Rapids, Mich.: Fleming H. Revell, Co. A division of Baker Book House, 1974).

Billy Graham, *Unto the Hills* (Dallas, Tex.: Word Publishing, 1996).

Liz Curtis Higgs, *Reflecting His Image* (Nashville, Tenn.: Thomas Nelson, 1996).

ACKNOWLEDGMENTS

Vickie Kraft, *Facing Your Feelings* (Dallas, Tex.: Word Publishing, 1996).

Max Lucado, *The Great House of God* (Dallas, Tex.: Word Publishing, 1997).

Max Lucado, *In the Grip of Grace* (Dallas, Tex.: Word Publishing, 1996).

Haddon W. Robinson, *Grief: Comfort for Those Who Grieve and Those Who Want to Help* (Grand Rapids, Mich.: Discovery House Publishers, 1996).

Robert Schuller, *The Be Happy Attitudes* (Dallas, Tex.: Word Publishing, 1985, 1996).

Andy Stanley, *Like a Rock: Becoming a Person of Character* (Nashville, Tenn.: Thomas Nelson, 1996).

Charles Swindoll, *David: A Man of Passion and Destiny* (Dallas, Tex.: Word Publishing, 1997).

Peter Wallace, *What the Psalmist Is Saying to You Today* (Nashville, Tenn.: Thomas Nelson, 1995).

Paul Walker, *How to Keep Your Joy* (Nashville, Tenn.: Thomas Nelson, 1987).

Laura Ingalls Wilder, *Words from a Fearless Heart*, ed. Stephen W. Hines (Nashville, Tenn.: Thomas Nelson, 1995).

Leslie Williams, *Night Wrestling* (Dallas, Tex.: Word Publishing, 1997).

Robert A. Williams, *Journey Through Grief* (Nashville, Tenn.: Thomas Nelson, 1991).

God's Love is

deeper than your tears.